Shades of Beauty

THE GLITTER GIRLZ SERIES

Written by Kelly Michele

Illustrated by Waqas Ahmed

IMAN FAITH
PRODUCTIONS
WRITERS COHORT

Copyright © 2021 Kelly Michele
Printed in the United States of America
ISBN: 9798509593918

The resemblance of any names or characters, businesses, or places, and events or incidents to actual persons, living or dead, or actual places or events is purely coincidental.

All rights reserved. No part of this publication may be reproduced, stored in a retrieval system, or transmitted in any form or by any means—electronic, mechanical, photocopy, recorded, or other—without the prior written permission of the publisher or Imani Faith Productions/Imani Faith Publishing. The only exception is brief quotations in printed reviews.

This manuscript is the property of Kelly Michele. Please do not duplicate or share without permission from Kelly Michele or Imani Faith Productions/Imani Writers Cohort.

Illustrated by Waqas Ahmed

Imani Faith Productions/Imani Writers Cohort
For more information on the Imani Writers Cohort or Imani go to: www.imaniwriterscohort.com

Acknowledgments

I first want to thank God for making all things possible, for without HIM I would not be who I am today. I also want to thank my family — Mom (Denise), Courtney, Cristen, Jayla, Kaelyn, London, Ena, Pat, Pinky, Chris, TJ, Jake, Barbara, Gloria, Chan, Lauren, & Adon. You have always been there for me, and you support and encourage me in everything I do! Thank you for being the ones I can always count on. My friends — Debbie, Rachel, Kim, Dionne, Stephanie, Neoshi, TJ (Girl), Tammy, Karen, Pat P., Ms. England, and Vi. You put up with my crazy ideas, and you love and support me through everything! I love you all! To Abby, Zurie, Harrison, Bria, Bakari, Jayden, and Shannon, Auntie Kelly loves you!

Special thanks to the Imani Writers Cohort and Dr. Kenneth Phelps.

Thank you to my readers. I hope my book inspires and encourages you. Your support means the world to me!

This book is dedicated to the loving memory of Dad, Nana, Grandpa, Grandmommie, Queenie, Uncle George, Uncle Ricky, and Little Ricky.

Preface

Shades of Beauty was born from a culmination of life experiences—from being teased about the lightness of my skin, to hearing a range of negative comments about skin tone, to kids making fun of classmates with darker skin. Unfortunately, perceptions about skin color, particularly that darker skin is ugly or inferior, continue to exist in society today. Throughout my career I have had students talk about how much they hate themselves because of their dark complexion. I have also had students question why they look the way they do, and they wonder why their complexion is different from their parents.

Just last month, something happened that truly broke my heart, and it still makes me sad. I was meeting with a student for our weekly social work session. That week, our school was hosting a virtual spirit week (our school is currently all remote), and she was dressed in the day's theme. She was excited about the way she followed the theme, and I thought she looked cute, so I asked to take her picture for the school website. Her mood instantly changed from cheerful to distraught. Her facial expression shifted, and she became visibly upset. "No, no, no!" she said. Of course, I respected her wishes and did not take her picture, but the social worker in me couldn't let it go. I began to explore the reason she felt this way. She told me she did not want her picture taken "Because I'm ugly." My heart broke, and I felt so sad that this beautiful girl really felt she was ugly. I probed a little further to understand more. She said she was ugly because her skin isn't fairer, and that if she were lighter then she would be pretty.

I wrote Shades of Beauty not only to help my student, but to inspire all children (and adults) and remind us all that our skin is beautiful in EVERY shade. I want them to know that there is no complexion that makes one prettier than another. It is my hope that this book will be a reminder that we are all beautiful!

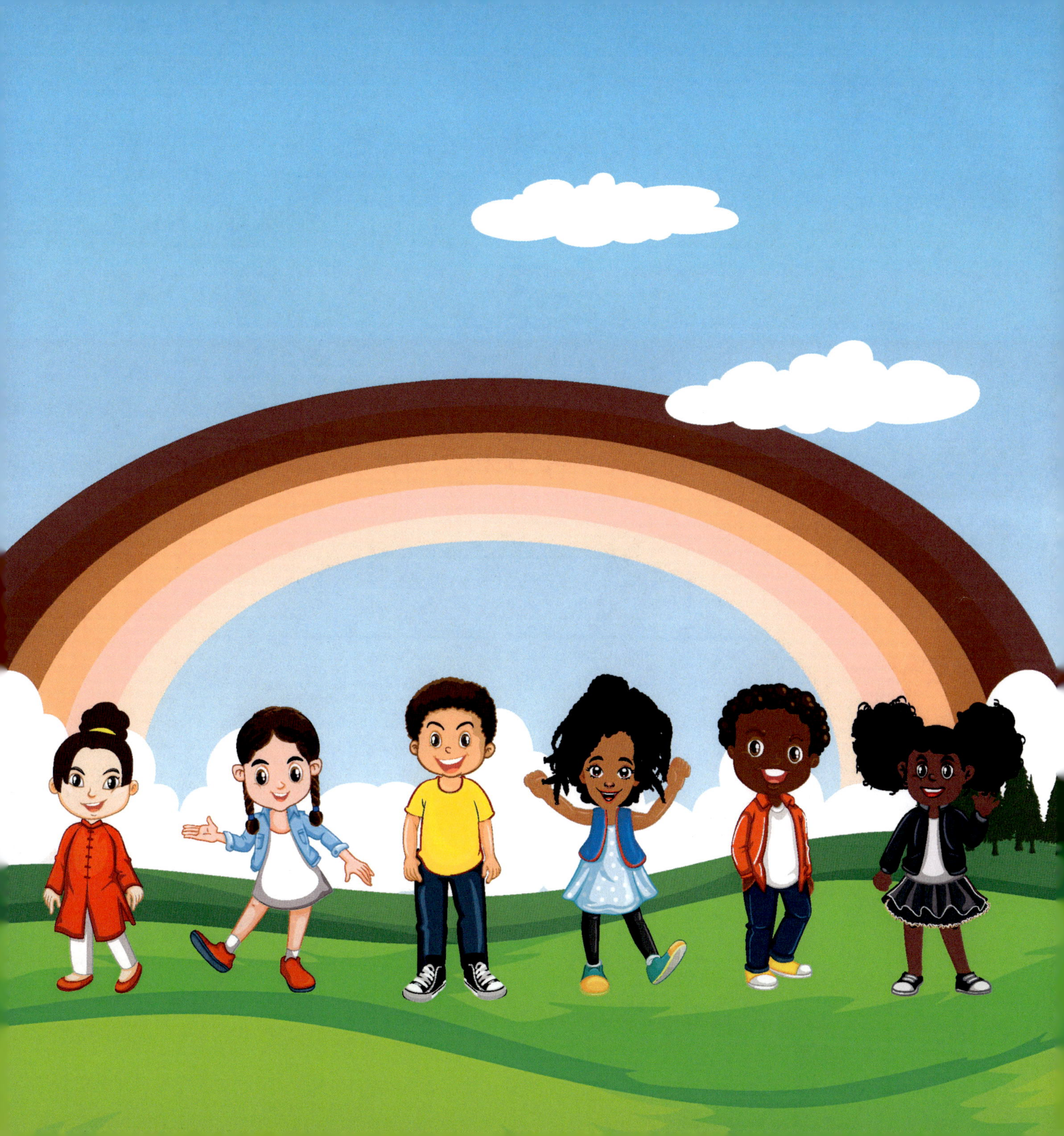

My skin is so light, almost transparent.
It's as if you can see right through me.

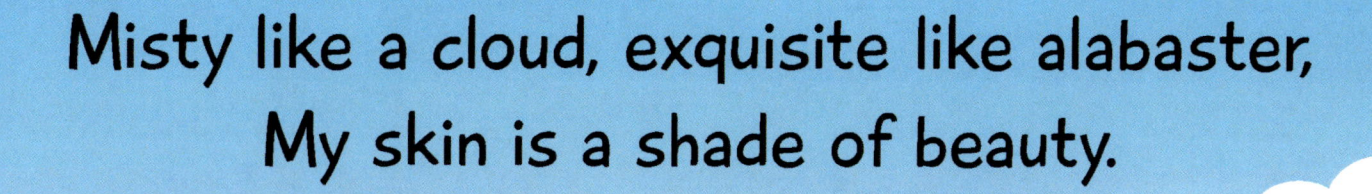

Misty like a cloud, exquisite like alabaster,
My skin is a shade of beauty.

My skin is pale pink, the color of blush,
Like an azalea, soft and sweet.

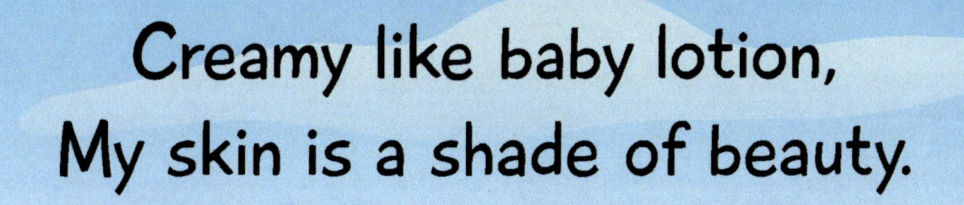

Creamy like baby lotion,
My skin is a shade of beauty.

My skin is beige, the color of wheat,
Like wind-blown sand,
flowing and free,

With a hint of red undertones,
My skin is a shade of beauty.

My skin is caramel, a lighter shade of brown,
Smooth like a piece of toffee.

It reminds you of warm apple cider.
My skin is a shade of beauty.

My skin is brown like cocoa.
Radiant, silk mahogany.

Rich like fine chocolate,
My skin is a shade of beauty.

My skin is dark brown, like coffee with no cream,
Strong like royalty.

Peaceful like the night sky,
My skin is a shade of beauty.

Light, pink, caramel, brown
Or any shade your skin may be,
You are beautiful and wonderfully made,
And your skin is a shade of beauty.

Affirmations

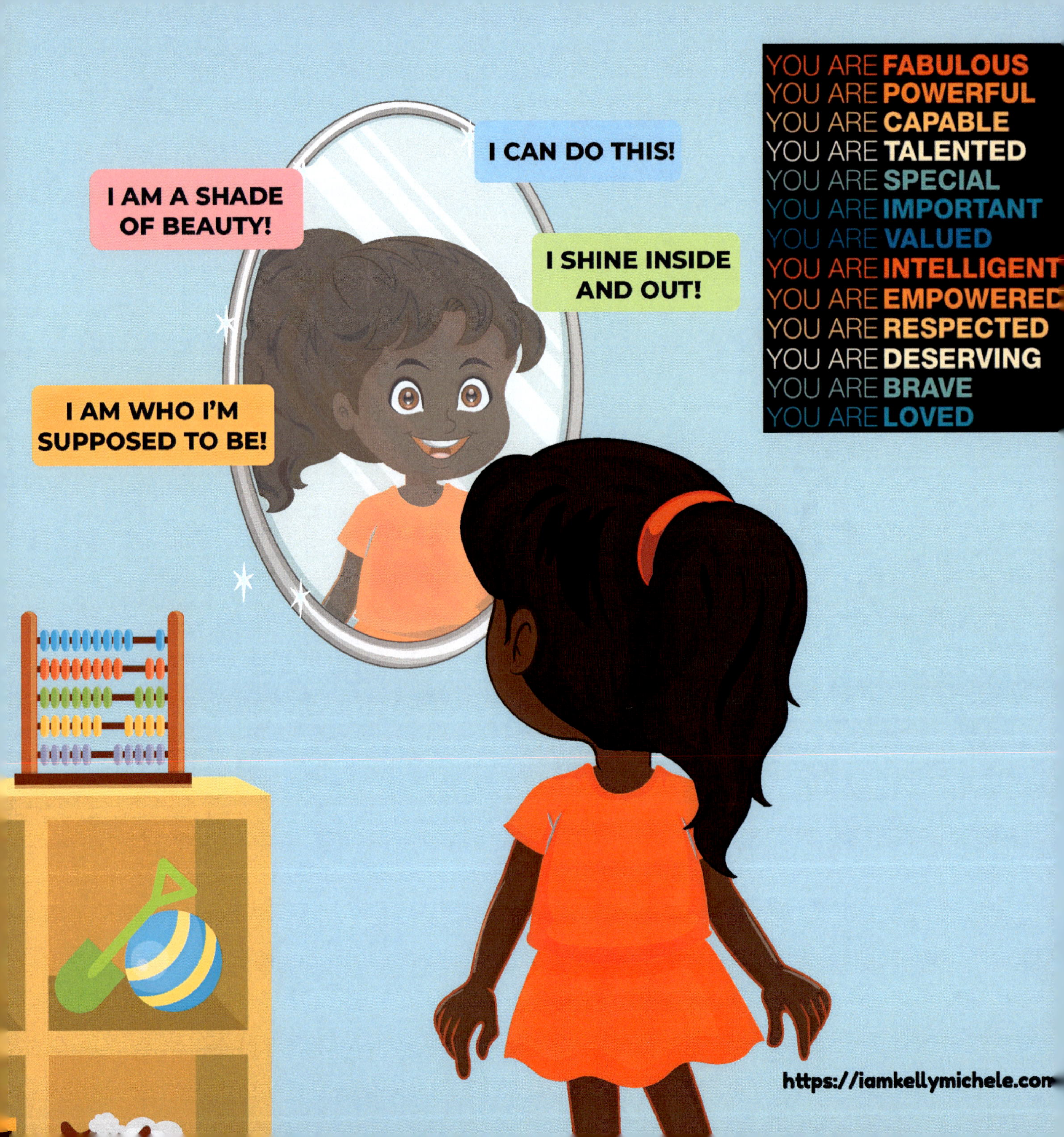

https://iamkellymichele.com

An affirmation is a statement or phrase you say to encourage or motivate yourself. It's also a way to declare something in your life. Affirmations are powerful. They steer our thinking, and our thoughts change how we feel about ourselves. Positive affirmations help increase our self-esteem. They help us get through challenging situations.

When they are practiced daily, affirmations can help us increase our self-worth. They can also help us defeat negative thoughts about ourselves and support a positive body image. At first, saying affirmations can feel awkward, but with practice you will become more comfortable. Here are four affirmations that can help you feel good about yourself, motivate you to do your best, and help you face challenging situations. Stand at the mirror and say each affirmation out loud. Over time you will notice how it becomes easier; it feels more natural. Parents of younger children, have your child look in the mirror and repeat each affirmation. It's never too early to begin this practice. Daily affirmations can give your child the tools they need to motivate themselves, manage anxiety, and boost their self-esteem.

Affirmation #1: I AM A SHADE OF BEAUTY!

This affirmation is a reminder that you are beautiful no matter what your complexion. There is no skin color that is more beautiful than any other. All skin is beauty!

Affirmation #2: I CAN DO THIS!

Life can be overwhelming. This affirmation is a reminder that you can get through it, one step at a time, one day at a time. You can do it!

Affirmation #3: I AM WHO I'M SUPPOSED TO BE!

It's a human tendency to compare ourselves to others. These comparisons can serve as motivation to improve, but can also make you feel inadequate. It's important to remember that you are unique—with skills and talents that make YOU special.

Affirmation #4: I SHINE INSIDE AND OUT!

This affirmation is a reminder that you are amazing! You have gifts and talents. You are special! It's also a reminder to do your best in all that you do.

Discussion Questions

Discussion Questions

1. How do you feel about your skin color?

2. Have you ever wished your skin color was different? If so, in what way?

3. Do you feel you have ever been treated differently because of your skin color? If so, talk about it.

4. Have you ever been teased about your skin color? If so, talk about it.

5. Have you ever teased another person because of their skin color? If so, talk about it.

6. Do you feel that your skin color matters? Why or why not?

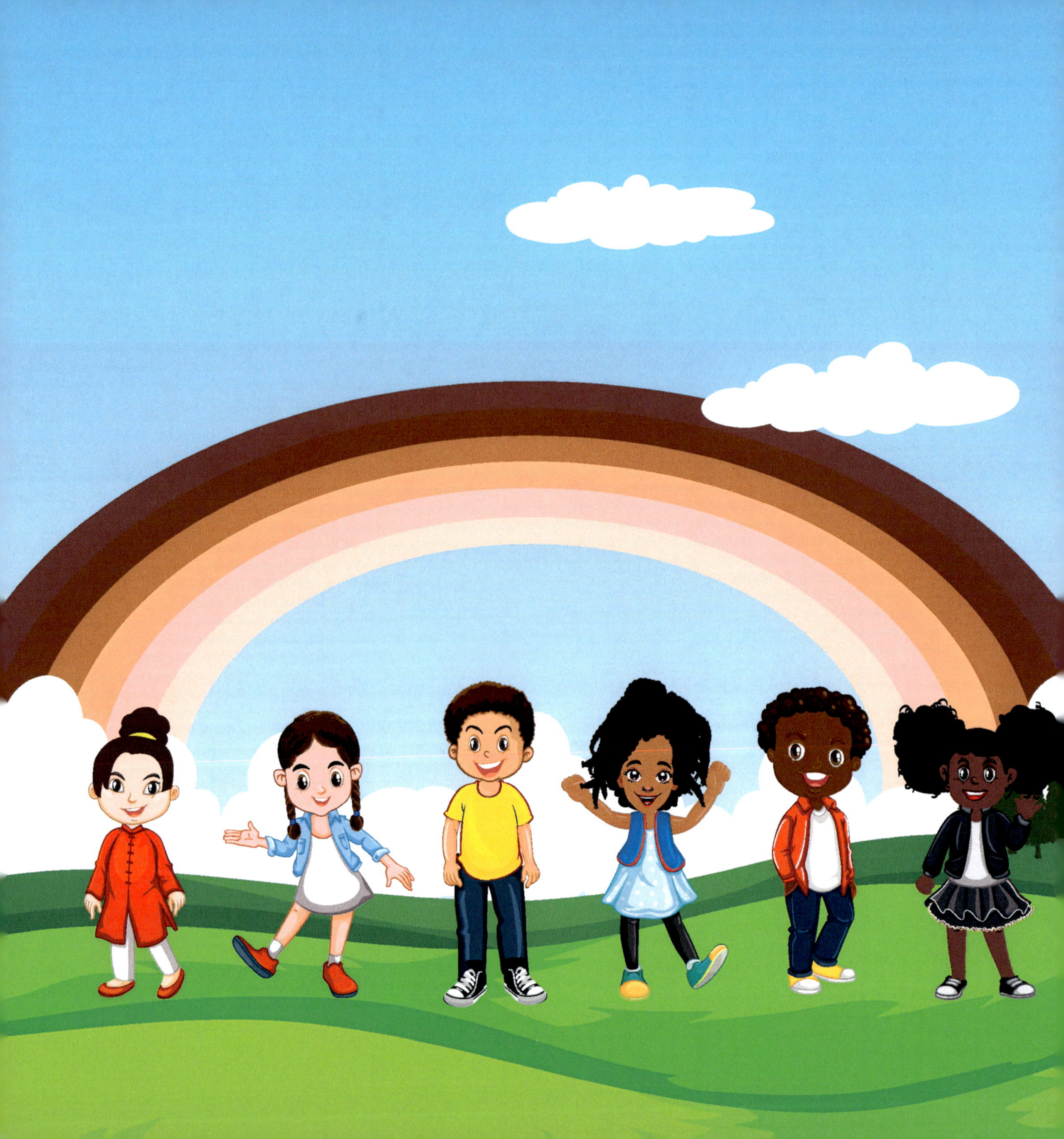

Activity

MY FACE

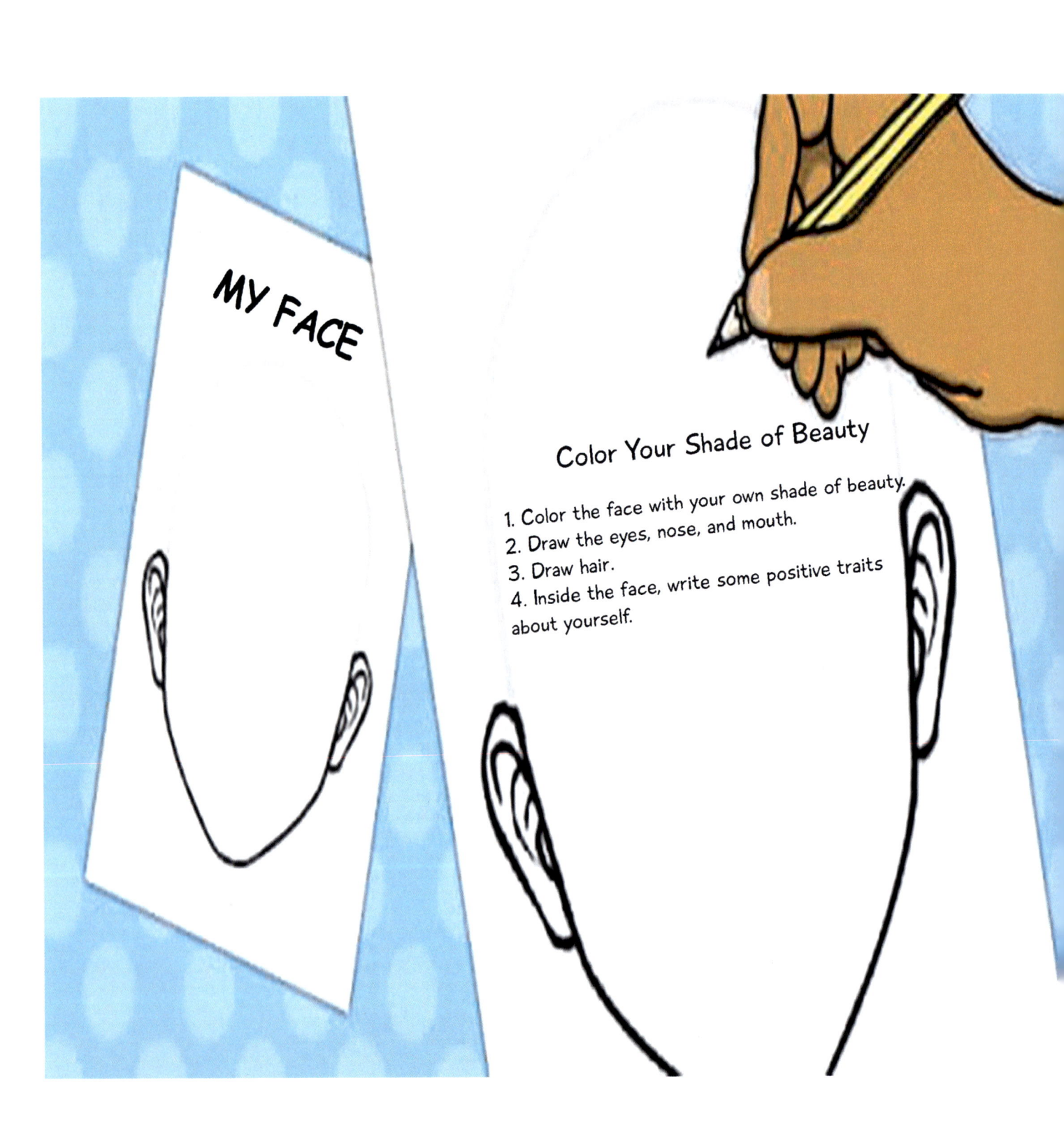

Color Your Shade of Beauty

1. Color the face with your own shade of beauty.
2. Draw the eyes, nose, and mouth.
3. Draw hair.
4. Inside the face, write some positive traits about yourself.

Color Your Shade of Beauty

About the Author

Kelly Michele is a proud alumna of Spelman College and the University of Chicago School of Social Service Administration. She holds a Bachelor of Arts degree and a Master's degree. She is a licensed clinical social worker and certified professional educator. Formerly a classroom teacher, Kelly currently works as a school social worker at a middle school in south suburban Chicago. Kelly loves to scrapbook and has a scrapbook picture frame business called Kelly's Keepsakes. She also loves to dance. Kelly is a former competitive dancer and dance instructor, and she is the Praise Dance director at her home church. Kelly has a four-legged "son," Reddy.

Kelly Michele is the author of That's MY Friend! (Imani Writers Cohort, 2019) and Cell Phone Drama (Imani Writers Cohort, 2020).

Contact Kelly Michele at iamkellymichele@gmail.com or find her online at www.iamkellymichele.com